Minding Mom

A Caregiver's Devotional Story

Lisa Livezey

En Route Books and Media, LLC
Saint Louis, MO

En Route Books and Media, LLC
5705 Rhodes Avenue
St. Louis, MO 63109

Contact us at contactus@enroutebooksandmedia.com

Cover Credit: Emilie Haney
Copyright 2024 Lisa Livezey

ISBN: 979-8-88870-280-2 and 979-8-88870-281-9
Library of Congress Control Number: 2024951511

Unless otherwise noted, all Scripture quotations are taken from the Revised Standard Version Bible, Catholic Edition. All rights reserved. No part of this book may be reproduced, stored in a retrieval system, or transmitted in any form, or by any means, electronic, mechanical, photocopying, or otherwise, without the prior written permission of the author.

To Dad, who trusted me to finish his work.
January 1, 1936 - September 24, 2017

To Mom, who counted on me to the end.
April 6, 1935 - September 23, 2018

Table of Contents

Foreword v

Prologue: Announcing Alzheimer's 1

Part I: UNEXPECTED FALL 3

    1. Sorry State 5
    2. Diligent Doctor 7
    3. Privacy Act 9
    4. A Savior Sighting 11
    5. Pop Star 13
    6. The Hallelujah 15
    7. Combatting Criticism 17
    8. Vital Sign 19
    9. Dawn's Early Sight 21
    10. Under the Old Oak Tree 23
    11. Single Song Sparrow 25

Part II: WEATHERING WINTER 29

    12. Serendipitous Surrender 31
    13. Assistance amid Resistance 33

14. Voice Over 35
15. Sharon 37
16. Pie and Goodbye 39
17. Caddy Back 41
18. Backyard Dash 43
19. Collecting Information 45
20. Adamas Anniversary 47
21. Yass Sister! 49
22. The Bleak Midwinter 51

Photographs 53

Part III: ETERNAL SPRING 65

23. Seeing Both Sides 67
24. Sister Act 69
25. Swearing on a Stack of Bibles 71
26. Bed Mime 73
27. Clothed with Humility 75
28. Dependent on Depends 77
29. Broken Body 79
30. Entering In 81
31. Almost Absent 83
32. Giving Back 85

Minding Mom: A Caregiver's Devotional Story   iii

Part IV: SUMMER DAZE 87

    33. A Pal's Eval 89
    34. Maybe Come Back 91
    35. Ensuring Good Health 93
    36. T.G.I.S. 95
    37. Dramatic Dahlia 97
    38. Perfunctory Prediction 99
    39. Artificial Intelligence 101
    40. Evaluation Brings Qualification 103
    41. From Boots to Armchair 105
    42. This Magic Moment 107
    43. Going with a Pro 109
    44. Two Moms and a Memory 111

Part V: THE FINAL SEASON 113

    45. Club Med 115
    46. Bed Climb 117
    47. Choosing Chocolate 119
    48. Placement Puzzle 121
    49. One Step Closer 123
    50. The Blues 125
    51. Buried Treasure 127

52. Caregiving 365 129

Epilogue: The Chosen Campground 131

A Note from the Author 133

Foreword

My wife and I first met Lisa years ago at church coffee hour and began a warm and lasting friendship. I remember clearly when Lisa assumed care of her mother who was in mid-stage Alzheimer's. Knowing the challenges of providing home care for someone with dementia, I kept Lisa in my prayers.

When Lisa requested an evaluation, we arranged a visit to her mother's home. What I encountered was a beautiful picture of loving care for a highly active 83-year-old senior with Alzheimer's dementia. Knowing that round-the-clock caregiving, even with hired help, is beyond a full-time job – and recognizing Lisa's many responsibilities in addition to her mother's care – I voiced honest concerns about burnout (#33, "A Pal's Eval").

Every caregiving situation is unique, but common challenges mark this daunting task which encompasses both hands-on care and administrative decisions for a loved one who is aging. I felt blessed to have had a small part in Lisa's journey and was encouraged to read these caregiving vignettes with accompanying scriptures and prayers.

Glory to God for this heartfelt devotional story which visits the day-to-day realities of caregiving and shows that God cares for the caregiver!

> Stephen Lybrand, M.A.
> Owner - Bennett, Shaw & Whitlock LLC
> Medicaid & Long Term Care Planners

Prologue

Announcing Alzheimer's

*Do not boast about tomorrow,
for you do not know what
any day may bring forth.*

—Proverbs 27:1 (NAB)

I stopped by my parents' split-level suburban home for a quick visit and Mom met me at the door. "Lisa, I have ALZHEIMERS!!!" she pronounced with angst. Dad stood in the background smiling tenderly. The news was no surprise. In fact, Mom had announced her diagnosis to me three times already.

In a flash moment, I considered Mom's exemplary life. She was a faithful wife, mother and grandmother, a registered nurse, volunteer librarian, had taken in foster children, kept an immaculate, organized home, and even led Bible studies. She doted on her grandchildren, who hold happy memories of time spent at "Gigi and Pop's" house and of weekends camping in the mountains.

Now at age 82, Mom was descending from the mountains and gazing despairingly upon the wilderness of Alzheimer's disease. For one so capable, no doubt the future appeared bleak and scary.

Giving her a hug, I said, "Don't worry, Mom. It'll be okay." Surely God would provide the daily help she needed, just as He had during her more productive years.

I knew Mom was in good hands with Dad's stabilizing presence beside her. He capably handled Mom's health issues and certainly would be her continued comfort and guide amidst the changing landscape of her brain.

Lord, Thank you for today.
I know not what tomorrow holds,
so help me to trust You with the future.

Reflect: Think about loved ones in your life who are experiencing change due to age or illness and offer up a prayer for each one.

Part I

UNEXPECTED FALL

1.

Sorry State

When Jesus saw his mother and the disciple there whom he loved, he said to his mother, "Woman, behold, your son."

—John 19:26 (NAB)

It was early Tuesday morning when I entered Dad's hospital room to find him awake. He had been hospitalized the day before and upon seeing me agonized, "I'm *so* sorry. Oh, honey. I'm *sooo sorry*, oh honey…"

Tears welled up within me, and I pushed words through the lump in my throat. "It's okay, Dad. I'll take care of Mom," I promised thickly. Despite this sudden turn of events, neither of us could have imagined that Dad's passing was just five days away.

I remembered a conversation two years back when I asked Dad, "What should I do with Mom if you die first?"

"Keep her at home, where she is comfortable," was his answer. But with Mom's fragile health, we both felt sure Dad would outlive Mom. He was Mom's rock—her guiding light amidst the darkening clouds of Alzheimer's disease.

I brought Mom to the hospital later that day. "Billy, what's going on?" she queried.

"Talk to Lisa," Dad managed to mutter. His speech capabilities were rapidly diminishing.

The caregiving mantle was being placed upon my shoulders. As I donned the weight of it, Dad's expression of heartfelt concern provided a comforting cloak. The memory of his love and life brought solace in the difficult days that followed.

> *Lord, help us to trust You in making*
> *the best decisions for our loved ones.*

Reflect: When did you first realize that you would be a caregiver? Close your eyes and thank the Lord for His faithfulness. Cast all your cares upon Him because He cares for the caregiver, too!

2.

Diligent Doctor

*"Write the vision;
make it plain upon tablets,
so he may run who reads it."*

—Habakkuk 2:2

There was a phone call from Alaska a couple months earlier notifying me that Dad had been hospitalized. While three days into a cruise with Mom, he had struggled to read his dinner menu and was admitted to the hospital in Juneau.

Dad had debated whether to take the cruise, worried about Mom's delicate health. After much deliberating and several doctor's visits, he had booked the trip—calling it their "Last Hurrah." Now *Dad* was hospitalized.

Several days of testing ensued, with Mom at his bedside. Images showed a dark spot deep in his brain, but without a biopsy, results were inconclusive. The doctor's notes quoted Dad: "I'm 81 years old and I've lived a full life. Besides taking care of my wife, I'm ready to go and don't want any invasive procedures—including a brain biopsy."

Dad was released from the hospital with instructions for follow-up care and appeared healthy upon his return home. Then two months later, in a doctor's office waiting room, Dad's words began faltering mid-sentence. I quickly wrote the date on a slip of paper and held it up. "Dad, what does this say?" He looked, paused, and then shook his head. The doctor rushed in, took a quick assessment, and called the ambulance.

At the hospital, Dad's motor skills declined rapidly, and doctors zeroed in on that spot deep in his cerebellum, wanting a biopsy. How thankful I was for that diligent Alaskan doctor whose copious notes provided clear confirmation of Dad's wishes.

*Thank you, Lord, for going ahead of us
and preparing the way.*

Reflect: Do you know the end-of-life wishes of your loved one? Ask the Lord to help you prepare both practically and emotionally.

3.

Privacy Act

*Their faces were turned away,
and they did not see their father's nakedness.*

—Genesis 9:23

It was a Tuesday evening when I encountered my younger brother in the hospital hallway outside the room where Dad had been admitted the day prior. He approached me, frustrated. "They won't tell me anything," he said. "*You* have to give them permission." As the person named by Dad to access his medical records, I needed to provide specific names of those who could receive information about Dad's condition. Stopping at the nurse's station, I gave approval that my brother's questions be answered and from then on, he barely left Dad's bedside.

Adopted by my parents at age four, my brother was thankful for Mom and Dad's provision of a stable home in time of need and was deeply bonded with Dad. I greatly appreciated his compassionate presence and emotional support at this time.

Entering the hospital room, I noticed Dad had loose pajama pants on beneath his hospital gown. Thus far, he had worn the standard hospital frock—tied at the neck and open down the back. The pants, although less convenient for hospital staff, offered coverage, and I felt a sense of relief at the increased decency. I later learned that my son-in-law insisted on this measure of propriety, advocating for Dad and thus protecting his dignity.

Thank you, Lord, for privacy measures and the protections they bring—both legal and physical.

Reflect: Think about the safety and comfort that privacy offers when you're feeling vulnerable. Are there ways to uphold your loved one's dignity? Ask God for the means and strength.

4.

A Savior Sighting

But we see Jesus, who for a little while was made lower than the angels, crowned with glory and honor.

—Hebrews 2:9

"It's Jesus, and it's so easy!" Dad pointed excitedly to the upper corner of the hospital room. This was the second time he had done so. What was he seeing? And what was so easy? Was there a distance he had to cross—something he had to do?

Dad had been hospitalized just two days earlier, but it seemed his earthly life was quickly waning.

His pastor visited that afternoon and concluded the final prayer with an 'amen.' Dad suddenly exclaimed, "Amen! So this is the end!" He was voicing acceptance of his fate and sounded excited about his future.

Yet by evening, things turned, and Dad became increasingly agitated. He fought to climb out of bed and morphine did nothing to subdue him. My brother and sons surrounded Dad's bed, physically grappling with him to prevent a headlong tumble over the bedrails onto the tile floor. The struggle continued for several hours until I finally headed to the nurses' station. "Something has to be done!" I insisted. "This situation is not sustainable." A doctor was called who prescribed different medication, thus effectively pacifying Dad and bringing relief to all.

Dad's earthly path was hitting some rough spots, but he now glimpsed his future and saw Jesus there—and it looked "so easy."

Lord, we want to see you, too.
Help us as we care for our loved ones
on this earthly journey toward heaven.

Reflect: What it would be like to peer into the next life and see Jesus? Tell the Lord how you would feel about seeing Him.

5.

Pop Star

*Grandchildren are the crown of the aged,
and the glory of children is their parents.*

—Proverbs 17:6

I stepped away from Dad's bedside as our eldest son pulled up a chair and spoke heartfelt words to his beloved grandfather. "Pop, thanks for taking me to lunch and for all the dinners at your house." My son continued to quietly, earnestly express thanks and love.

Dad was affectionately known as "Pop" to all our children. He loved his grandchildren deeply and for years had incorporated them into his joyful Christian existence.

Pop, in retirement, was the self-proclaimed "chief cook and bottle washer" of his household. To this day, our kids reminisce about his delicious spaghetti, morning pancakes, and buttery popcorn served warm from a large brown paper bag.

Pop often invited his grandchildren to accompany him to an inner-city ministry where he performed Bible stories for the students. Sometimes, our phone would ring the night before with Pop asking about a certain stuffed animal, a staff, or some other prop he hoped to use in his amateur production the next morning. One of our children often accompanied him, playing parts like the shepherd, wise man, or woman at the well.

Although Pop was leaving us, his loving care and the memories he created would remain in the hearts of his devoted posterity.

*Lord, thank you for loved ones
who structure our lives with
truth, love and joy.*

Reflect: Do you have childhood memories of a loving grandparent or teacher? Thank the Lord for that blessed one.

6.

The Hallelujah

Once more they cried, "Hallelujah!"

—Revelation 19:3

It was Friday, and Dad had been moved to the hospice unit on the hospital's sixth floor. Out-of-town family members were filtering in to pay their last respects.

After Dad was admitted the previous Monday, the nurse handed me a plastic drawstring bag which held the clothing and shoes he'd been wearing upon admission. At the bottom of the bag was Dad's wallet. It felt so personal, looking through his wallet. Therein, I found a well-worn paper which unfolded to show a handwritten list of Christian songs. I began calling this "Pop's Playlist." My daughter found the songs online and assembled a digital recording which we began playing in Dad's hospital room.

Meanwhile, Mom wandered down the hall looking for her husband. "Do you know where Dad is?" was her refrain. She even wrote a message on the whiteboard in his room: 'Dear Billy, I'm here looking for you… Your love.' It was heart-wrenching.

The music playing in Dad's room offered comfort, hope, and fellowship to all who entered, and we assumed Dad could hear it as well. One song included was the "Hallelujah Chorus" from Handel's *Messiah*. That afternoon as the chorus sounded, Dad belted out a single, "Hallelujah," in tune with the music. It was the last word he ever uttered.

> *The hallelujah has possessed my soul,*
> *to You, O Christ, I give my praises all.*[1]

Reflect: Read or listen to Revelation 19. Picture yourself among the worshippers at the marriage supper of the Lamb. Interested in knowing the songs on "Pop's Playlist?" Email me for the list: lisa@lisalivezey.com

---

[1] "Tydi a Wnaeth Y Wyrth, O! Grist, Fab Duw / Pantyfedwen." https://www.musicanet.org/robokopp/welsh/tydiawna.htm.

7.

Combatting Criticism

For behold my witness is in heaven, and he that knoweth my conscience is on high. My friends are full of words: my eye poureth out tears to God.

—Job 16:19, 20 (DRB)

The news spread about Dad's condition and visitors began pouring in—fellow choir members, church friends, extended family, and many people that Dad and Mom had helped over the years.

There was Matt, whom Dad helped find employment and paid the application fee for refinancing his home. And Constance, whom we'd all grown to love—a graduate student who lived with my parents for several years. In walked Yun, a nurse Mom had befriended at work decades earlier. Then there was Clark, who received help more recently, but whose integrity I questioned and whose presence as a house guest Mom thinly tolerated.

I headed down the hospital hallway Saturday afternoon in search of coffee only to encounter Clark.

He began questioning me about Dad's care, aggressively insisting that something could be done to save him. *Weren't things hard enough already?* I finally interrupted him, saying, "I can't have this conversation right now, Clark." A nurse working nearby heard me and glanced up—our eyes met. Yes, we all were in shock. Even a distant relative had called the hospital, questioning the doctor about Dad's quick decline. Everything had happened so fast, but the reality was that Dad was dying.

Lord, enable me to act wisely in every situation and keep me strong when I'm doing my best and others are questioning me.

Reflect: Think about your initial reaction when criticized about your caregiving decisions. Remember that God sees you and loves you. Ask Him for wisdom, thank Him for those critics, and pray for them.

8.

Vital Sign

The LORD will give you a sign.

—Isaiah 38:7 (GNT)

It was a September Sunday morning at 2 a.m. when I descended the hospital elevator and stepped out through sliding glass doors. Walking to the nearby corner, I bought coffee at the 24-hour convenience store. The warm cup soothed my palm as I continued around the block, taking comforting sips of the hot liquid. It seemed surreal that only a week ago Dad had been living his full, active life.

A woman stood on the opposite sidewalk tossing pebbles up against a second story window, trying to awaken the sleeper inside.

There was a sleeper inside of me resisting all this change. What was I going to do with Mom, and how could I manage everything on top of my own full life? I told Dad years ago that if he went first, I'd keep Mom at home where she was comfortable. But was that truly possible?

I rounded the corner and started up Main Street, lined with silent boutiques and artisan coffee shops. Suddenly ahead of me appeared a sign, brightly lit. In bold black letters were the words, FEAR NOT, I AM THE ONE WHO HELPS YOU. Was I dreaming, seeing this sign in the middle of the night? No doubt it was a message from God that He saw me and would help in the coming days. I took a picture, found courage in the moment, and headed back towards the hospital.

Thank you, Lord, for giving us signs–
especially in times of desperate need.

Reflect: What signs of encouragement has the Lord given you along your caregiving road? Keep a watch this week for evidence of his loving care.

9.

Dawn's Early Sight

Arise! Shine, for your light has come,
the glory of the LORD has dawned upon you.

—Isaiah 60:2 (NAB)

I returned to the hospital room early Sunday morning, September 24th. It was dark, and the only sound was Dad's loud and steady breathing. My brother and oldest son were asleep nearby on cots.

On Friday I had leaned over, hugged Dad and told him I loved him, hearing a muffled, "Love you, sweetie," from deep within. It was our last interaction. Sitting now at Dad's bedside, I lowered the rail and rested my head upon his chest. His heartbeat was steady, but I knew the time was short and expected him to pass that afternoon.

Outside the sun was rising and during its ascent shone directly through the window onto Dad's face. Glory's doors were opening, and it seemed that heaven's Light was welcoming Dad.

Just then, I detected a change in Dad's breathing. Still steady, it had developed a hollow sound—the end might come sooner than I thought. Hurriedly, I phoned sleeping family members. My brother and son awakened from their cots and stood vigil at the bedside. My sister arrived with Mom in tow. Dad had been waiting. Two minutes after Mom reached his bedside, Dad entered his new dawn in heaven.

Overnight, I had assumed four new titles: Executrix, Trustee, Power of Attorney and Personal Representative for Mom.

Lord, arise and show me Your glory as I step forward into the responsibilities You have placed before me.

Reflect: How is the Lord shining His light upon you today? Ask Him to be a lamp unto your feet and a light upon your path.

10.

Under the Old Oak Tree

*They may be called oaks of righteousness,
the planting of the Lord, that he may be glorified.*

—Isaiah 61:3

The weather had been sunny, warm, and dry all week. I parked along the edge of the meandering cemetery road and exited the car, walking past the weathered sign that marked the section leading to Dad and Mom's grave plots. 'The Garden of the Gospels,' the sign read, a fitting theme for Dad and Mom. Navigating between dozens of grave markers, I reached the middle area and found the flat grassy area which soon would be Dad's gravesite.

A towering oak tree stood nearby, its branches reaching far and wide in all directions. I lay on my back, feeling the warm grass beneath me, and gazed skyward through tree branches at the meandering clouds. Such a huge tree—and it had all begun with a single acorn.

I considered the many seeds of help, hope and love that Dad and Mom had planted throughout their lives—now mature and producing fruit. There were the missionaries they'd supported over the years, the women in the Bible studies that Mom had led, the people Dad had helped as a church deacon, the children at the inner-city missionary school where they volunteered weekly, the list went on and on.

Even though Dad was now gone, his influence surely would bear fruit for generations to come.

Lord, thank you for the righteous examples of people who serve You. Help me to follow You with my whole heart.

Reflect: Take a deep breath in and let it out. Offer up your caregiving to the Lord remembering that each day you are planting seeds of love.

11.

Single Song Sparrow

*Are not two sparrows sold for a penny?
And not one of them will fall to the ground
without your Father's will.*

—Matthew 10:29

Dad's funeral. We sat in the fourth pew with Mom, except now Dad was absent from his usual spot in the choir loft. Our daughter, a professional violinist, played a beautiful tribute to her beloved grandfather. Standing on stage with long blonde hair flowing down her back and graceful arms poised, she sounded the strains of a much-loved hymn. I pondered the words as she played.

*Why should I feel discouraged, why should the
    shadows come,
Why should my heart be lonely, and long for
    heav'n and home,
When Jesus is my portion? My constant Friend
    is He:*

His eye is on the sparrow, and I know He watches me.

Never before had I heard the song played so poignantly as the moving strains culminated in a sweet crescendo.

Following the final prayer, my sister and I walked Mom back up the aisle. I was grateful that Sis would remain in town for a couple weeks while I managed the deluge of details following Dad's death. But then she would fly back to her home out west.

"Let not your heart be troubled," His tender word I hear,
And resting on His goodness, I lose my doubts and fears;
Though by the path He leadeth, but one step I may see;
His eye is on the sparrow, and I know He watches me...[1]

---

[1] "His Eye Is On The Sparrow," a hymn written in 1905 by Civilla D. Martin and Charles H Gabriel.

Within the myriad of decisions confronting me, I could trust Jesus to lead me through each one.

> *Thank you, Jesus, for watching over us*
> *as you do the song sparrow.*

Reflect: Think about how Jesus is watching over you. Lay aside any doubts and fears and rest in His goodness.

Part II

WEATHERING WINTER

12.

Serendipitous Surrender

It is the Lord who goes before you;
He will be with you.

—Deuteronomy 31:8

I slipped into the quiet Adoration Chapel, seeking blessed respite from the frenzied pace which now characterized my days. Tucked among the prayer cards in my Bible were some papers which, when unfolded, brought back a sudden memory.

These had been handed to me in this very chapel by an older woman who often prayed there. It had been a month ago when she approached me as just the two of us were sitting in the chapel. Holding out some papers, she had whispered, "I feel like you're supposed to have these."

I accepted them with a quiet, "Thank you," honored that this prayer warrior had singled me out. The title read *Novena of Surrender to the Will of God* and was followed by nine daily prayers, each ending with the words: "Jesus, I surrender myself to You. Please take care of everything." I began the first prayer immediately and planned to continue for the next eight days.

When the weekend arrived, I forgot all about the *Surrender Novena*. Then came Monday afternoon—and then Dad was rushed to the hospital—and then he died—and then I became responsible for Mom.

In rediscovering these papers, I realized that the Holy Spirit had nudged this holy woman, causing her to give me the *Surrender Novena* just days before my life was about to radically change.

Jesus, I surrender myself to You.
Please take care of everything.

Reflect: Focus on the Lord and purposefully repeat the above prayer ten times. If able, search online for the *Novena of Surrender to the Will of God* (Author: Father Don Dolindo Ruotolo 1882-1970) and pray it for the next nine days.

13.

Assistance amid Resistance

*Listen now to my voice; I will give you counsel,
and God be with you!*

—Exodus 18:19

"I love you with the love of Jesus, Beth." Miriam beamed at Mom and leaned towards her. Mom stared back stonily.

I'd first met Miriam at Mom and Dad's house a couple years earlier. A church friend, originally from Kenya, Miriam embodied the joyful, vibrant faith I often noticed in African Christians. She was a regular at my parents' kitchen table and had paid an emotional bedside visit to Dad at the hospital.

Miriam worked in a nearby retirement community and offered to help us on her days off. I gratefully accepted. Always friendly to Miriam in the past, now Mom was resistant. She pressed her lips together the moment Miriam entered the room. Eventually, Mom's temper flared. "It's MY house!" she yelled and glared at me with a clenched fist held high above her head. Then she faltered, letting her arm drop.

"Yes, it's your house, Mom, and I'm trying to keep you here." I stated resolutely.

Thankfully, Miriam's caregiving experience helped her not take things personally and the advice she offered was invaluable. She bought thick, waterproof pads for Mom's bed, advised on hourly rates for private-pay aides, and suggested keeping a daily logbook of Mom's care.

Ultimately, Mom never did accept Miriam, but I'm thankful for the experienced help in those early days. Miriam's upbeat attitude and timely advice provided solid ground when everything around me was shifting.

Lord, I need Your help in this new season of life. Thank you for bringing along experienced people to advise me.

Reflect: Who has been especially helpful in your caregiving journey? Ask the Lord to bless that person and if possible, thank them personally.

14.

Voice Over

My sheep hear my voice,
and I know them,
and they follow me.

—John 10:27

"Billy? Billy??" Mom sat in her chair at the kitchen table calling Dad's name.

"He's not here right now, Mom," I said truthfully. She accepted this news placidly and returned to eating her cereal.

I remembered Mom turning to me while standing beside Dad's hospital bed a couple months earlier. "He has a drinking problem," Mom had whispered confidentially. I chuckled despite the sadness of the moment. To Mom, the person in the hospital bed had become "the man from church."

I hadn't realized how much Mom depended on Dad's confident, cheerful voice to guide and orient her. Once his voice faded, she no longer recognized him. In some ways, it softened the impact of the moment, and for that I was grateful. Now with Dad gone, the voice Mom heard was mine, but it didn't sound—or feel—the same as her husband of 59 years.

Truth be told, I too desired Dad's strong, kind voice to guide me in making decisions on Mom's behalf. Instead, I was listening to wise, experienced counsel and praying for guidance. I purposed to surround Mom with sounds of love and be a voice advocating for her when she could no longer do so for herself.

*Lord, let me hear Your voice as I seek
to follow You in making wise decisions.*

Reflect: What experienced voices are available to help in your caregiving journey? In addition to those voices, rest in the comfort and love that comes from the Lord through His words in Scripture.

15.

Sharon

A friend loves at all times.

—Proverbs 17:17 (NRSVCE)

"I want to help," wrote Sharon in her email.

Sharon and her husband Sam met my parents fifteen years earlier when attending a new church. Dad and Mom were the first people to greet them and immediately invited them over for a meal.

Sam was a scientist at Johnson & Johnson and Sharon was working in home health care. Her email came weeks after Dad died, offering help at a time when I sorely needed encouragement.

Sharon became a dependable aide. Punctual, helpful, and kind, she always greeted me with a wide, beautiful smile. She came alongside Mom as a true friend, going above and beyond the basic expectations. Sometimes she brought food to cook, and other times offered helpful suggestions for easy, inexpensive meals. Something as simple as a packet from the supermarket that could be mixed up into mashed potatoes provided an easy lunch or dinner.

I heard recently that the name 'Sharon' originates from Hebrew and means "from fertile fields and forests." Sharon's help felt like bounty straight from the hand of God. She was an aide to Mom, yes, but even more a true friend who helped uphold Mom's dignity and quality of life when Mom could no longer do so for herself.

Thank you, Lord, for sending quality friends to help—a provision straight from Your hand.

Reflect: Is there a special friend in your life or the life of your loved one who is especially helpful right now? Thank the Lord for His provision and thank that person for their friendship.

16.

Pie and Goodbye

*Everything that happens in this world
happens at the time God chooses.*

—Ecclesiastes 3:1 (GNT)

It was a dream birthday celebration for me. My two beautiful daughters arranged brunch at a local restaurant, and when I arrived, three of my closest friends were there waiting! The six of us sat at a round wooden table near the window, enjoying artisan offerings of eggs and charcuterie. The morning sun shone in, warming my shoulders as these loved ones warmed my heart.

My older daughter lives overseas, so her presence made things extra special. My younger daughter, an artist, had baked and brought my very favorite—a cherry pie topped with latticework crust, using Dad's recipe. After clearing our plates, the server brought the pie with candles ablaze. Closing my eyes, I thanked the Lord for this amazing time. I felt so special.

Buzz-buzz. I reached for my phone. It was Mom's morning aide, Zola, her voice desperate. "Your mother has locked me out of the house and won't let me back in!!!" I hurriedly thanked my daughters and friends, pushed back my chair, and rushed off to Mom's house.

Not seeing anyone outside, I raced to the patio door only to discover that Mom had finally decided to grant Zola entrance.

Shortly thereafter, my daughters arrived, and we all sat at Mom's kitchen table eating delicious homemade cherry pie, feeling thankful that the emergency happened towards the end of my birthday brunch. The interruption was a stark reminder of my new normal, but the silver lining was that Mom enjoyed eating pie along with us.

Lord, we know not what will happen next, but we trust You anyway, both now and for the future.

Reflect: Think back to a birthday in which you felt especially loved. Thank the Lord for those who made it special.

17.

Caddy Back

*My lord, thou knowest that I have
with me tender children.*

—Genesis 33:13 (DRB)

Outside Mom's house sat three vehicles. There was the 26-foot camper parked near the patio, the old gray Buick Century Sedan that Dad had used around town and kept running with duct tape and spit, and finally the tenth-generation beige Cadillac de Ville—reserved for more dignified occasions.

Soon after Dad died, my son—savvy with Craigslist—helped sell the Buick for several hundred bucks. As for the camper, winter wasn't the best time to sell. Plus, I lacked the time and energy just then to clean and empty it out. Then there was the Caddy which offered a quiet, padded ride—like sitting in the lounge of a fancy hotel.

Despite the Cadillac's availability, we had been chauffeuring Mom to daily activities in my car or that of her aide. But when riding shotgun, Mom was tense and frequently burst forth with exclamations of dismay at the mere passing of another car.

I discovered that if Mom sat in the middle of the Cadillac's backseat, she would ride contentedly along in peace. Thus, I didn't sell the Cadillac and began driving Mom around in the vehicle where she felt most comfortable. It was Mom's car, after all, and hers to enjoy.

Lord, we are but weak children.
Thank you for Your provision of tender care.

Reflect: Is there something in your loved one's life that provides physical comfort? Is there a tangible way in which God shows His tender care for you? Take a moment to thank the Lord for His provisions.

18.

Backyard Dash

I have been terribly worried trying to find you."

—Luke 2:48 (GNT)

I dropped my son off at art class and the call came. "I can't find your mother!!!" Zola burst out desperately. "She left the house, saying that she wanted to walk to your house *alone*. I followed her in my car, but now I can't find her!"

I made a U-turn and accelerated towards Mom's neighborhood. To reach my house, Mom would have to walk across a busy two-lane road.

Zola's car was pulled over a half mile from Mom's house on a side street. She hurried towards me, distressed, pointing towards where she'd last seen Mom disappear into someone's backyard. I walked down the short driveway of an unknown neighbor and scanned the yard. "Mom? Mom? Are you here?" No answer. A garage and thick trees were behind the house with tall hedges along the driveway. Mom was nowhere to be seen.

I walked to the front door and knocked. It was 1:00 p.m. on a weekday. A middle-aged man wearing large wire-framed glasses opened the door. "Is my mother in there?" I burst forth, worriedly.

He stood looking at me, a smirk on his face. I suddenly realized how ridiculous this must look and sound. In a flood of words, I explained the situation. Then, he joined the search party.

After another five minutes of calling and looking, I noticed a slight impression in the bordering hedges. Drawing closer, I pushed through the thick pine branches, "Mom? Mom?"

At the sound of my voice, came her wavering response, "Lisa?" And then I spotted her, disheveled and distraught, at the corner of the next yard. Upon seeing me, she began to cry. Poor Mom. I hugged her, thanked the neighbor, and soon we were home in Mom's familiar kitchen making a cup of tea.

Thank you, Lord, for guiding us in unexpected situations.

Reflect: What has been your craziest caregiving experience? Who helped you at the time?

19.

Collecting Information

He who planted the ear, does he not hear?
He who formed the eye, does he not see?

—Psalm 94:9

Mom wasn't feeling well, and seeing no obvious signs of illness, I suspected another urinary tract infection (UTI). An historically chronic issue for Mom, if not treated immediately, a UTI would progress to a bladder infection and make her very sick.

With it being a weekend, we visited the local pharmacy's walk-in clinic. The nurse recognized Mom, saying that my father had brought her in several times for the same problem. "She needs to see a urologist." She spelled it out for me, "U-R-O-L-O…"

In Dad's file drawer at home was a thick manila folder labeled, "Beth's Medical Care." Thumbing through it, I learned that Mom had seen a urologist regularly in the past. Why had Dad been taking her to the walk-in clinic? Well, at least I had a solid lead for a specialist.

The urologist visit resulted in medical oversight from a kind, competent nurse practitioner who understood the constancy of Mom's UTI's. Over time, she pragmatically worked out a helpful system for me. I was provided with a stack of sterile specimen cups and lids, and whenever a UTI appeared to be developing, I collected a clean specimen from Mom. Then, I delivered the specimen discreetly in a labeled paper bag to the front desk of the urologist office. From there, an antibiotic would be ordered if necessary.

Practical arrangements like this were godsends when managing Mom's care, and I was most grateful for the kind pragmatism of that nurse practitioner.

Lord, thank You for Your help, even in small details, thus making the caregiving burden lighter.

Reflect: In what details of your caregiving do you see the hand of God through the kind help of others?

20.

Adamas Anniversary

For he is the living God, enduring for ever;
his kingdom shall never be destroyed.

—Daniel 6:26

On December 21st, six decades ago, Mom and Dad had gotten married. I remember as child looking at their black-and-white wedding photos and hearing Mom say the bridesmaids' gowns were a brilliant green. I remember one hanging in the attic, of shiny green taffeta, and pictured the wedding party posing amidst dozens of red and white poinsettias at the front of the church. It must have been a beautiful sight!

This year would have been my parents' sixtieth anniversary, known traditionally as the Diamond Year. The word diamond comes from the Greek word "adamas" meaning unconquerable, enduring, indestructible. Indeed, Dad and Mom's marriage had endured the test of time—for richer, for poorer, in sickness and health, and only through death did they finally part.

In past years, we joked about the calendar date of Mom and Dad's wedding—winter solstice—the longest night of the year. But this year Mom's sixtieth anniversary found her alone—a widow. Rather than this night feeling long and emotionally difficult, dementia was kindly easing Mom's grief.

For my parents' anniversary the previous year, I had purchased a gift certificate to a nice restaurant in town. Both in their eighties, neither needed a walker or cane and their health appeared to be holding up well. With Dad alongside her, Mom navigated life seamlessly to the outside observer. Little did I know that soon things would change! How glad I am now to have facilitated a dinner date for their last wedding anniversary together.

Lord, thank you for marriages that stand the test of time. Thank you that Your love is diamond-like—adamas—unconquerable, enduring and indestructible, far beyond this earthly life.

Reflect: Think of ways that God's love has proven itself "adamas" to you.

21.

Yass Sister!

Her children show their appreciation.

—Proverbs 31:28 (GNT)

After my father's funeral, my sister stayed with Mom for a few weeks before flying back to her home out west. Her timely help was a true godsend. The difference in our personalities shone through in the ways we cared for Mom.

Sis bought a huge pot for the stove and began brewing herbs reputed to cure Alzheimer's disease. That was fine by me, but I was not one to stir up stovetop concoctions.

My approach focused more on keeping a healthy schedule and diet for Mom, finding loving caregivers, and preserving her dignity by keeping her dressed nicely with hair styled.

Every morning after helping Mom get dressed, I blow-dried her hair using a round brush. It was like she had a personal hairstylist.

As Christmas approached, my sister offered to stay with Mom for a few weeks, giving me a blessed reprieve. How nice it was to have my mornings back, and Mom was thrilled to have to have Sis there by her side.

When Sis and Mom arrived at my house for Christmas brunch, I chuckled inwardly. Mom was dressed so differently from what I would have chosen, and her hair—although clean—was lying a bit flat atop her head. Mom, of course, was oblivious to these details. She was comfortable and happy, her inner core satisfied with my sister's companionship and attention to her needs.

*Thank you, Lord, when siblings support
one another in caring for a loved one.*

Reflect: Think of ways that you have worked with a relative or friend to help another person. Pray a blessing today for that co-caregiver.

22.

The Bleak Midwinter

For it is the God who said, "Let light shine out of darkness," who has shone in our hearts.

—II Corinthians 4:6 (NRSV)

My eldest son John, bless his heart, moved into a bedroom at Mom's house and monitored her overnight activity. He also offered to shovel in the event of snow, but thankfully it wasn't a snowy winter. That was fine with me because snow—despite its beauty—would add chores and challenging road conditions to the daily caregiving duties.

Teeth chattering as I arrived at Mom's house early each morning, I thought of the poem "In the Bleak Midwinter" by English poet Christina Rosetti which speaks of "frosty wind made moan." Despite this year's lack of snow, the line "snow on snow, snow on snow" somehow described my daily caregiving grind.

Rosetti's poem concludes with heartfelt words expressing worship and sweetness surrounding the birth of the Christ child:

> *If I were a shepherd*
> *I would bring a lamb,*
> *If I were a wise man*
> *I would do my part,*
> *Yet what I can I give Him,*
> *Give my heart.[1]*

Within my own inner struggles during this difficult season, I sought to give Christ my heart. And despite Mom's jumbled mind, one thing that never wavered was her heart's devotion and love for Jesus.

> *What can I give You, Lord?*
> *I give you my heart this day.*

Reflect: Are you feeling inner desolation surrounding the constant caregiving? Offer up your suffering heart as a gift to the Christ Child.

---

[1] Rossetti, Christina. "In the Bleak Midwinter." Poetry Foundation, 2022, https://www.poetryfoundation.org/poems/53216/in-the-bleak-midwinter.

Photographs

#1. Unexpected Fall—
Mom and Dad's last Christmas together in 2016

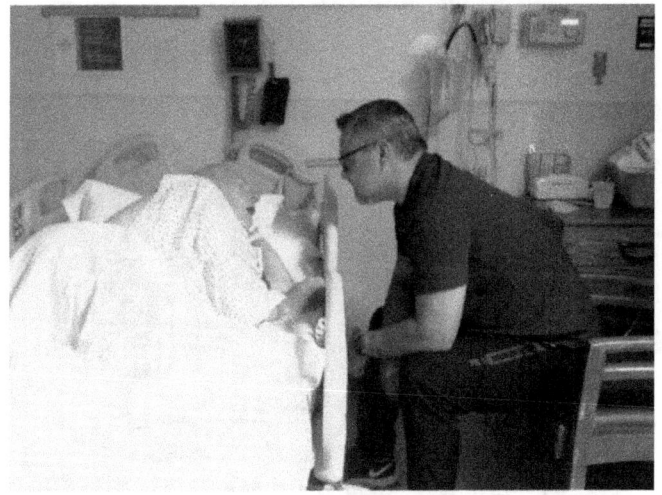

#3. Privacy Act—My sweet brother at Dad's bedside

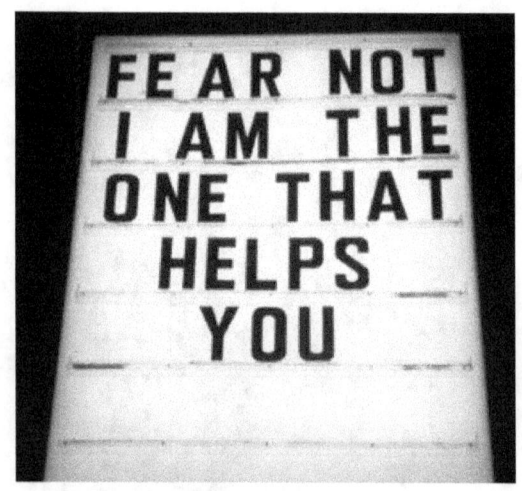

#8. The vital sign

#11. Bronwyn (stage right) played the violin at her grandfather's memorial service

#15. Sharon giving loving care to Mom

#16. Mom, friend Monica, Yours truly, friend Lorrie, and daughters Bronwyn (pie maker) and GlenFern. Baby Samuel (right) was born in the blue room one month before Dad passed away

#24. Mom with her sister Ruthie, and family friend Jeannie

#27. Mom all dressed up and enjoying some tea

#32. The only (very-grainy) photo I could find of Mom and me during our 365 days together

#36. Thank God for Kira

#37. The Dramatic Dahlia

#38. Mom (an hour after predicting her own death) with dear friend Trudy

#42. The Great Trevini

#43. Mom and Dad's house

#44. Two moms and a memory, August 18th

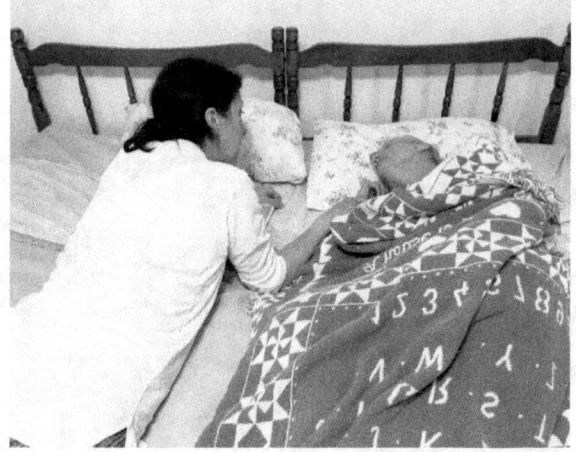

#49. Mom's faithful evening aide, Joann, helped me get her upstairs the last time

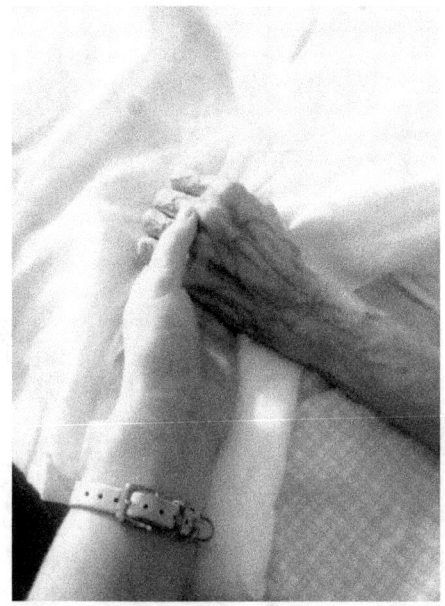

#51. Buried treasure

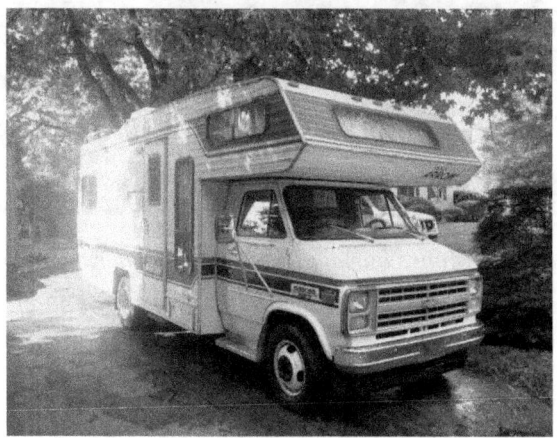

*Epilogue. My parents' happy place—
their 26-foot Tioga Arrow camper*

Dad and Mom's burial place, located under the old oak tree (see p. 23), I sometimes go there to reflect and pray.

Part III

ETERNAL SPRING

23.

Seeing Both Sides

First sit down and count the cost.

—Luke 14.28

In the months following Dad's death, Mom complained that she couldn't see very well, and I thought her eyeglass prescription might need some adjustment. The ophthalmologist suggested surgery for one eye, saying it would provide greater clarity.

I went through a mental debate surrounding Mom's quality of life and the progressing Alzheimer's disease. How much time did she have left? How well could she tolerate eye surgery in the midst of mental disorientation? The financial cost would be high, but Mom had good health insurance. What about the recovery period when she would be under strict post-operative guidelines?

I deferred the surgery, opting instead for a stronger prescription for her glasses. As we selected frames for Mom, I considered buying two pairs. She often misplaced her glasses around the house. The cost of one pair was several hundred dollars—did I want to double that cost just for a backup pair? I chose the more conservative route by ordering just one set of frames, thinking her old glasses could be the backup pair. A second pair of new frames, and the eye surgery, could wait for now.

In the end, my gut assessment proved right. Putting Mom through surgery would have been deeply unsettling for her. As the Alzheimer's approached later stages, it went into rapid decline and Mom stopped wearing her glasses altogether, not even missing them.

Making decisions on Mom's behalf wasn't always simple, but God's grace was sufficient each step of the way.

Help us, Lord, to accurately count the cost monetarily, physically and emotionally as we make healthcare decisions for our loved one.

Reflect: What decision are you facing right now within the care of your loved one? Write down the pros and cons of each choice and pray for wisdom.

24.

Sister Act

Now there stood by the cross of Jesus his mother, and his mother's sister.

—John 19:25 (KJV)

Mom was extremely active physically, and I was continually searching for ways to fill the time. Her younger sister Ruthie also suffered from Alzheimer's and spent her days at an adult daycare. I tried signing Mom up for the same daycare, but she wouldn't tolerate the setting.

I pictured Mom and Ruthie together in past years—at the beach, going to birthday lunches, and working on cross-stitch samplers in Mom's living room. Perhaps Ruthie could visit Mom at home once per week.

My uncle agreed to bring Ruthie to Mom's house on Friday mornings. She shuffled mechanically through the door grasping my uncle's arm, hardly the same person I remembered playing tennis and riding her bike around town.

Mom's Friday aide was a friend who had stepped in for a short while to help. A couple weeks into this arrangement, she informed me that compensation for taking care of two people should be higher than the rate for just Mom. I appreciated her candid honesty, having not even considered this fact. I figured that adding Ruthie to the mix would ease the situation because she sat placidly at the kitchen table and her presence reined Mom in.

The arrangement didn't necessarily make things easier and in time came to an end, but I don't regret the effort. The sisters met weekly for several months, and the final Friday that they spent together marked their closing sisterly act on earth. Ruthie has recently passed from this life, and I now enjoy the thought of the two sisters together in heaven.

Thank you, Lord, when a sister's companionship can continue throughout the years.

Reflect: Is there a relative the person you're caring for would like to see? Ask God to show ways for facilitating a visit.

25.

Swearing on a Stack of Bibles

For the Lord is a God of knowledge,
and by him actions are weighed.

—I Samuel 2:3 (NRSVCE)

My mother wasn't known to swear. Her words had always been more scripture-oriented than drawn from the gutter. As a child, I remember her reading the *Scofield Reference Bible*, and in more recent years it was her *NIV Study Bible*, marked with underlining and notes in the margins.

I recalled only once ever hearing Mom cuss in my presence when we were returning from a family vacation. As our station wagon rounded the final corner towards home, we saw our 1970 Chevy Nova there in the driveway seriously smashed up. My older brother hadn't accompanied us on vacation and conveniently wasn't home just then.

"He'd better get his @#% home," I remember Mom saying. I'd never heard her talk that way before and was taken aback. But that was forty-some years ago.

In this current season, spring yard cleanup was underway, with my supportive and helpful husband busily raking Mom's yard. Suddenly, she emerged from the house and purposefully headed towards the neighbor's car, attempting to open the door. "That's not your car, Mom," my husband stated matter-of-factly. Mom turned towards him with fire in her eyes and said definitively, "d#%* you!"

To this day, we chuckle about the moment and the person for whom she saved the expression. Alzheimer's was removing some of Mom's mental filters, but her swearing moments remained few and her love for scripture foremost.

Lord, thank you for Mom's lifetime of God-focused living and thank you, too, for the humorous moments sometimes brought on by dementia.

Reflect: What is your loved one doing that is funny and might be different from their norm? Allow yourself to laugh.

26.

Bed Mime

In peace I will both lie down and sleep.

—Psalm 4:8

I didn't know Mom was a stomach sleeper until the last year of her life. At bedtime, I would walk with her to the bathroom sink and hand her a warm, wet washcloth with which she dutifully scrubbed her face. Next, I would load the toothbrush with toothpaste and give it to her. She diligently and vigorously gave her teeth a thorough brushing. Although she taught me how to brush my teeth as a child, I realized now my current toothbrushing pattern was cursory compared to hers.

Next, I'd assist Mom with her nightgown. A night*gown*—not pajamas. In winter, it was a flannel nightie—usually white with a delicate floral blue pattern. In summer, it was a sheer, short-sleeved shift in pastel pink or green.

Once Mom was ready for bed, I would pull back the covers and watch as she climbed in, listening to her express how good it felt to get into bed. I would adjust the pillow and watch her turn and get settled on her stomach. There was a specific way she placed her right hand up near her face and slid her left arm down alongside her body. Once Mom positioned herself that way, I knew sleep would soon follow.

There's an intimacy in knowing whether someone is a stomach sleeper, side sleeper, or back sleeper. These were things I'm sure Dad knew well, but now I was learning them about Mom.

> *Thank You, Lord, that You know*
> *our ways completely.*

Reflect: What special things have you learned about your loved one while caregiving? Cherish the intimacy and thank the Lord for the privilege of knowing.

27.

Clothed with Humility

*Yea, all of you be subject one to another,
and be clothed with humility.*

—I Peter 5:5 (KJV)

It was 7 a.m. when I arrived at Mom's house, saying both good morning and goodbye to my son as he headed off to work. I walked through the kitchen and up the short flight of steps to the hall of Mom's split-level home. Reaching the landing, I could see Mom through the open bedroom door, sitting on the edge of the bed sporting a creative, comical combination of clothing. She wore a shirt, with two bulky sweaters layered over top and the second sweater was on backwards. Her slacks were pulled on, and she was attempting to tug a pair of pantyhose over top of them.

"Need a hand, Mom?" I asked her. She looked up with an expression of frustration on her face, aware that something wasn't quite right. Chuckling a bit, she willingly accepted help as I gently removed the sweaters and the twisted stockings. I was reminded of the sweet humility that resided deep inside Mom's spirit. It surfaced when her way of doing things wasn't working.

I hope that aiding Mom each day helped me cultivate some inner humility, and I pray to inherit the same sweet spirit, should one day I be the one needing help.

Lord, please allow humility to develop within me and thank you for those who exhibit godly examples of this honorable trait.

Reflect: Do you feel like your caregiving experience brings opportunity for humility? Offer up those humbling moments to God.

28.

Dependent on Depends

She brought her wagons and loaded them too.

—Judith 15:11 (GNT)

I was never one to frequent the drugstore, but as a caregiver, shopping at Rite Aid became a regular routine. Keeping my mother's prescriptions filled was one reason, but also the constant need for adult incontinence underwear. A single package held 16-count which, with doubling up at night, lasted several days. When they were on sale, I stocked up and could vouch for best variety: Depend Night Defense!

Standing in the pharmacy line one morning, I recalled a scene thirty years prior while waiting in a similar cue. The woman ahead of me, probably in her fifties, was buying Depends. I wouldn't have noticed her merchandise, except that she repeated several times to the clerk, "They're for my mother." In my twenties at the time, this woman's need to explain her purchase enlightened me about something I'd never considered: Seemingly healthy people might be incontinent.

Now, that fifty-something woman buying Depends was me—and I promise they really were for my mother. But instead of just one package, my cart held three. Suddenly aware of my complete lack of embarrassment, I pondered my psyche and realized that humiliation was the least of my worries these days. *Who cares if the person in line behind me thinks I need to wear Depends?* I was just blessedly relieved when the store had ample supply and even better, when needed items were on sale. I depended on Depends all day and night for Mom and couldn't risk running out.

Lord, thank you for Your mercy which shows itself in practical ways, like the invention of Depends.

Reflect: What practical items ease your daily caregiving journey? Name them and thank God for them.

29.

Broken Body

He broke it and said,
"This is my body which is for you."

—I Corinthians 11:24

She wasn't Catholic in the least, my mother, but attending her own Presbyterian church was becoming problematic. When Dad was living, he kept an eye on Mom from up in the choir loft as she sat there in the fourth pew.

Now without Dad, Mom was increasingly restless at church even with familiar people nearby and an aide in tow. When she refused to get into the car after church one Sunday, requiring deacon involvement, I knew a change was necessary.

If Mom had realized that I was bringing her to a Catholic church, her mind would have been clouded by preconceived prejudices. But Alzheimer's filtered out these biases as I led Mom into mass the following Sunday. She sat obediently beside me in the last pew.

As the organ played and the faithful stood to reverently make their way up front for Holy Communion, Mom was captivated. Sensing the deeply spiritual moment, she gazed upon those in line, and whispered, "Beautiful."

The rhythmic words of the priest floated through the church, reaching us in the last row. "The body of Christ. The body of Christ. The body of Christ. The body of Christ." The beauty, truth, and goodness of the moment penetrated through disease and reached Mom's soul.

Thank you, Jesus, that within our brokenness you give us the miracle of Your broken body in Holy Communion.

Reflect: Has your loved one been to church recently? Have you?

30.

Entering In

For I am the Lord, and I change not.

—Malachi 3:6 (DRB)

Mom and Dad's house was my dwelling place from the tender age of two until I got married, minus a couple years at college. When pulling into the familiar driveway, I would exit the car and walk to the right side of their 1950's split-level home where the curved flagstone walkway met the patio. In autumn, I watched the ground, careful not to twist my ankles on "monkey balls" deposited by the towering tree alongside the driveway. The patio itself once boasted the same decorative flagstone but now was poured concrete, providing a place to park the camper. From the patio, I accessed the house's side door—wooden and painted yellow, with thick glass on the upper half. Mom preferred this door for family and friends alike and we called it the "back door." A curtain covered the glass on the inside, offering privacy from the knocking visitor.

I found the keyhole to be stubborn even when using the correct key. Over time, I learned to press in the key ever-so-slightly, turn it gently to the right, and twist the knob simultaneously. Then, the door would open easily.

I would enter, absorbing the familiar pleasant scent of the family home, and deposit my shoes on the mat to the right. Knobby Berber carpet met my stockinged feet as I walked through the rec room and ascended the six steps to the kitchen.

I had entered this patio door thousands of times over the years. Now, the familiarity brought comfort to what was becoming a new normal.

Lord, in changing times, help me to remember that You alone are unchanging.

Reflect: What is it about God's constancy that most comforts you?

31.

Almost Absent

Beareth all things, believeth all things,
hopeth all things, endureth all things.

—I Corinthians 13:7 (DRB)

May 31st marked our thirty-second wedding anniversary. Thinking back two years to our thirtieth anniversary, it all made sense now. My dear husband David had planned a surprise anniversary party for me. He rented out a cozy local venue and invited many a long-time friend.

After I walked in and heard the initial "SURPRISE!" a pause ensued. Then, I noticed Mom and Dad off to the right, looking a bit disheveled as if they'd dropped everything at a moment's notice. Dad was wearing his daily khaki shorts and a rumpled t-shirt and Mom wore her casual slacks and blouse—definitely not party clothes.

Later, I put two-and-two together. David had sent email invitations, and in the busyness of planning, with it being a surprise (and perhaps because I tend to be the social planner in our house), Dad and Mom weren't aware of the party. Apparently, my daughter noticed their absence and called them minutes prior to my arrival at the party.

Administrative details like checking emails, paying bills, and managing the social calendar had always been Mom's jurisdiction, but now these were falling to the wayside. Dad was overwhelmed as he managed everything around the home and emails were left unopened.

I'm so grateful to my daughter for noticing my parents were missing and for making that phone call. It was a blessing to have Mom and Dad at our thirtieth anniversary party!

*Thank you for precious memories
that we can hold onto when big changes occur.*

Reflect: Think of a gathering from the past when your loved one was present. If able, reminisce about it with him or her.

32.

Giving Back

The LORD sustains him on his sickbed.

—Psalm 41:3 (NAB)

"It's terrible, what I'm doing to you," Mom said as I tucked her into bed. "But I don't know what to do about it."

In that brief moment, Mom recognized the effort her care was requiring. It was a stark minute of reality as the unforgiving Alzheimer's disease marched on. Mostly, Mom seemed oblivious to the demands the illness was placing on those around her.

"It's okay, Mom," I said.

Was it really okay? I asked myself. I was doing what was best for Mom—doing what she wanted by keeping her at home. Sometimes, she articulated her wishes, but most often not. Mom had provided healthcare directives, so I had clear guidelines. The part about staying in her own home wasn't part of those directives; however, it clearly was Mom's place of comfort, and Dad had wanted her kept at home. I knew Mom's heart—how much she loved her home, her church, and how she appreciated seeing the grandchildren. By God's grace, I hoped to represent her needs and wants accurately.

Yes, my life had been interrupted in huge ways. But Mom and Dad had fed and clothed me for many years when I was young and had been amazing grandparents to my children. Now it was my turn to give back.

Lord, thank you for lucid moments that help us feel seen. But no matter what, thank you that You see our labors and they are not in vain.

Reflect: Does it feel like your life has been interrupted by caregiving? Ask the Lord to sustain you in this difficult season.

Part IV

SUMMER DAZE

33.

A Pal's Eval

"What you are doing is not good. You and the people with you will wear yourselves out, for the thing is too heavy for you."

—Exodus 18:17,18

I contacted my church friend, Steve, who worked for a company that offered on-site consultations to those caring for an aging loved one at home.

Steve arrived on a Sunday afternoon—Mom and I met him at the door. Although Mom didn't know why he was there, her antennae were up. Saying she didn't want to intrude, Mom descended the six steps to the rec room as Steve and I sat at the kitchen table.

Eventually, I checked on Mom and found her trying to listen in while simultaneously "organizing" the room. Books and videos were strewn everywhere. "Mom, would you like to join us?" I asked.

"I want to give you privacy," she answered. I welcomed her up to the kitchen.

Mom sat at the table, eagerly listening as Steve discussed assisted living options. Suddenly, she reached across the table to me, "We can do this, Sis!" she said eagerly. *Hmmm,* I thought. *Does she think we are siblings discussing options for a parent, or is she trying to tell me something?*

Steve and I finished and stood up as he gathered his papers. As we walked towards the door, Steve lowered his voice and offered his initial take on things.

"Your Mom is doing well," he said, "But it's full-time work for you amidst your own full-time life and family." He promised a follow-up email containing a summary and recommendations.

Thank you, Lord, for kind friends who provide knowledgeable, unbiased advice.

Reflect: Are you weary from your full-time caregiving work on top of your own full-time life? Know that God sees you laboring in the trenches and pray for wisdom.

34.

Maybe Come Back

He is a merciful God. He will not abandon you.

—Deuteronomy 4:31 (GNT)

Mom perched on the edge of the bed and patted the mattress, beckoning to me. I sat down beside her, unprepared for her next words: "I thought we had an agreement," she said.

"What do you mean, Mom?" I asked. It seemed that our afternoon meeting with the senior care consultant had her worried. *No, we didn't have an agreement,* I thought. *Dad wanted you to stay at home, and I'm trying. I'm really trying, but it's taking a heavy toll on me and my family.*

Mom was unable to further articulate her thoughts, so I tucked her into bed, pulled the sheets over her shoulders, and gave her a kiss. "See you in the morning, Mom," I said and kissed her forehead.

She looked up at me. "Will you really come back?" she asked. I assured her that, of course, I would return in the morning as usual.

Chatting briefly with my son on the way out, I said goodnight and then left. While driving home, I thought about Mom. *Doesn't she know by now that she can count on me? Oh well, she'll have forgotten by morning.*

But Mom's memory held firm. As I turned my key in the doorknob early the next morning, I saw her through the glass, parting the curtain, and peering out worriedly. She was up and waiting for me!

"You came back," she said as I stepped inside. "I didn't think you would."

Lord, we are frail in our humanity. Please instill within us the assurance of Your constant presence, despite what we might feel or what others may think.

Reflect: Close your eyes and rest in the mercy of God, knowing that He will not abandon you.

35.

Ensuring Good Health

He will ensure my safety and success.

—2 Samuel 23:5 (NLT)

Mom was a registered nurse back in the day, and her last job before retirement was working at a local nursing home as evening supervisor. I remember her pushing a bulky cart down the long hallway as she distributed medication. Some patients would receive a liquid diet supplement called Ensure. Mom opened the can with a pointed metal opener and poured the thick creamy liquid into a cup, handing it to the patient to drink.

Fast forward forty years, and now I'm managing Mom's care at home. Although she couldn't always express feelings of hunger, she was a good eater and downed her three daily meals quite readily. Afterwards, she willingly took the pills that I placed before her in a small cup.

At Mom's doctor appointment, we found she had lost several pounds, and I didn't know why or how.

Was she eating less? Exercising more? I pondered things, prayed for wisdom, and suddenly remembered Ensure. Having no idea of its taste, I bought some anyway.

In the midafternoon, I tried giving Mom a cup of Ensure. It was thick and sweet and even came in flavors—chocolate or vanilla. I didn't name the drink, in case it would trigger a memory and cause Mom to balk. I just said, "Mom, I have a milkshake for you." She took the glass of Ensure and gulped it down quite happily. With this new daily diet supplement, Mom soon was back to her standard weight.

Thank you, God, for pre-arranging every detail needed to help us care for our loved one.

Reflect: Are there any health details in your loved one's care that need added wisdom? Ask the Lord to provide helpful solutions.

36.

T.G.I.S.

At the seventh time he said, "Look, a little cloud no bigger than a person's hand is rising out of the sea."

– I Kings 18:44 (NRSVCE)

I woke up two minutes before the alarm went off. 6:28 a.m. How I wished just once to have a lazy morning. But caring for Mom didn't allow for a break; she always needed someone there. The pace was relentless – day in, day out—with Sundays often the hardest days, as availability of her regular aides was scarce on weekends.

I mentally reviewed the schedule for the zillionth time. A week totaled 168 hours. My son took the overnight 63, with hired help covering 65 weekday hours, plus my 14 morning hours. That still left 26 waking hours of care on the weekends.

"Kira wants to help," the text said. My sister-in-law's daughter, Kira, was a student in nursing school. Relief flooded me as I thought of having Sunday help. Daring to hope, I immediately replied, "Yes."

From that point forward every Sunday morning, young cheerful Kira arrived bringing fresh energy to the house, a kind spirit to Mom, and sweet relief to me. I could attend church unencumbered and enjoy a few hours of respite. On Sundays, I would awaken, knowing I had the morning free and would say outloud, "T.G.I.S. Thank God it's Sunday!" .

*Thank you, Lord, for providing relief
just when we most need it.*

Reflect: Are you feeling weary from the daily demands of caregiving? Ask the Lord to provide some refreshment.

37.

Dramatic Dahlia

And from His fulness we have all received,
grace upon grace.

— John 1:16

I noticed it in the neighbor's yard near Mom's house—a giant flower blooming upon a single tall stem. It was unlike any cultivated flower I'd ever seen. Peach in color, it had straight, pointed dense petals that radiated up and out to result in a huge blossom the size of a dinner plate.

Although this immense bloom stood near other flowering shrubs, its dramatic size captured the onlooker's gaze. I'd never seen anyone working in the yard but was tempted to knock upon the door just to find out the variety of this stunning stroke of nature.

You can imagine my surprise the next afternoon, after walking through Mom's rec room and climbing the six steps to the kitchen to find that very same flower standing in a vase on the kitchen table. Mom's aide Joann stood at the counter preparing an afternoon snack for Mom, and she filled me in.

On their daily walk, Mom and Joann had shared friendly conversation several times with the neighbor in whose yard the flower grew. It was he who had picked this masterpiece and chosen to bestow it upon my sweet, Alzheimer's-stricken mother. The gardener gave the best flower of all to Mom.

Lord, thank you for choosing the most fragile among us to receive the greatest graces.

Reflect: Can you think of a time when someone brought you flowers or fresh garden produce? Think about the fragrance or the taste, appreciating God's goodness in those moments.

38.

Perfunctory Prediction

A garment of praise for the spirit of grief.

—Isaiah 61:3 (DRB)

I returned to the car after pumping gasoline, and Mom piped up from the backseat. "You know what? I think I'm gonna die soon!"

Shocked, I turned and asked her why.

"I don't know. I just think I am," she stated matter-of-factly, nonplussed.

We were driving some forty miles to a retirement community where Mom's friend Trudy lived. Trudy and Mom had formed their friendship sixty years earlier when working together as hospital nurses.

Once at the retirement community, we navigated the hallway maze to Trudy's room. Displayed neatly on the door were the names: 'Frank and Trudy K.' I remembered Mom's joy years ago when Trudy had married Frank, the loving husband she truly deserved.

A nurse saw me knocking and waved us in. Past the kitchenette and into a tiny living room, we found Trudy and Frank stationed in padded chairs watching television. Trudy lay in a special recliner, her legs extended. Her body couldn't stand up to receive Mom, but her spirit danced about. She spoke excitedly with us. After six decades of friendship, this might be Mom and Trudy's last visit. Frank smiled, his eyes moist with the significance of the moment. For Mom, dementia softened this reality, and Trudy's personality didn't allow for opining. Both Mom and Trudy were happy, enjoying the inner bond of deep, lasting friendship. The onlookers, Frank and I, witnessed the delight of their friendship and allowed it to lift our garment of heaviness.

*Lord, thank you for joy that comes
from friendship amidst the realities of life.*

Reflect: Think of a friendship that brings you deep joy. What about that person that lifts your spirits?

39.

Artificial Intelligence

*You shall not turn aside to the
right hand or to the left.*

—Deuteronomy 5:32

My parents had neighbors, Larry and Dee, kind supporters of Dad in later years and timely help during the chaos following Dad's death.

Another bordering neighbor was Vince the plumber. Vince was quiet and kept to himself, but he would wave hello when we saw him outside. A couple years earlier, Dad had installed a decorative "friendship fence," as he called it, to shield the piles of plumbing equipment stashed alongside Vince's house.

Larry and Dee knew a young couple looking for a home in the neighborhood. I agreed to show them Mom's house, stipulating that it wasn't immediately available. If the couple had serious interest, we could arrange a future purchase once the house was empty.

Given the hot real estate market, it seemed prudent to take this opportunity and perhaps prevent the need to list Mom's house later.

Word travels fast in a neighborhood. The next day as I walked up the driveway, Vince approached me. "What's up?" he asked and then launched into a speech about keeping my mother at home until she died. I said little but thought about armchair quarterbacks versus the players sweating on the field.

Nothing came from the showing, and when the sewer clogged some months later, Vince kindly came to the rescue—and even gave me a discounted price.

Lord, thank you for well-meaning people.
Give me patience when I'm criticized, and please
bestow upon me wisdom for the decisions ahead.

Reflect: Are there decisions you currently face regarding your loved one's assets? Ask the Lord for an extra measure of wisdom and protection when facing a barrage of advice from others.

40.

Evaluation Brings Qualification

He will be our guide even unto death.

—Psalm 48:14 (KJV)

"Have you considered hospice?" the nurse asked. *Hospice?? Mom could run circles around me. She wasn't anywhere near needing hospice.*

I was having my mother evaluated for placement in a residential care facility. Even with all the outside help, keeping Mom in her own home was taking its toll on me and my family. So, it seemed best, after the year mark of Dad's death, to find a new place for Mom. *At least then I'll know I kept her home for a year*, I consoled myself.

The nurse examining Mom at the care facility assessed her as borderline for assisted living and informed me the memory care unit was full. Then, she asked if I'd considered hospice and recommended a few providers. That was on Wednesday.

Thursday, I called one of the recommended hospice companies, and on Friday they came to Mom's home for an initial assessment. I followed the nurse outside afterwards, not wanting Mom to hear our discussion. We sat on the flagstone steps that led to the front door, the sunshine warming our shoulders. The nurse confirmed that Mom qualified for hospice, due to her dementia.

"So, when will she be on hospice?" I asked.

"She's on it," the nurse stated confidently and kindly.

And that was it. Providential provision of a nurse manager visiting weekly, an experienced aide for one hour on weekdays, and a steady supply of medication to keep Mom calm and comfortable.

*Thank you, Lord, for opening
the hospice doors at just the right time.*

Reflect: How are you doing as you care for your loved one? Would there be reason to schedule a free hospice evaluation? May the Lord show you His best way.

41.

From Boots to Armchair

*Do your best to win full approval in God's sight,
as a worker who is not ashamed of his work.*

—II Timothy 2:15 (GNT)

Following the hospice decision, rumblings sounded from those "not in the game." I journaled this letter, not to send, but for personal processing.

Dear Armchair Quarterback,

It's me—here on the playing field. The effort is nonstop in this final quarter of a season that began years ago.

I wipe my sweaty brow and picture you sitting comfortably, life unchanged, beverage of choice in hand. You call the other armchair to talk. Perhaps strategy of play is discussed, analyzed, and the final score debated. I consult a coach and keep up the pace, running, pressing on—not wanting to quit, but wondering how long before the final buzzer sounds. Can I maintain this speed?

I see outside Mom's kitchen window a sturdy grape arbor covered with vines, industriously planted long ago. The gardener has gone away, but the arbor remains, and the vines are overgrown. I don boots and gloves, working to prune, protect, and fertilize using the best methods of care. The effort is intense, and the labor is constant. Careful tending promises a sweet harvest. A protective netting covers the arbor to stave off wild birds. There should be plenty of ripe grapes ready for distribution at harvest time. I pray there isn't a Monday morning storm, for that could cause good fruit to fall to the ground, wasted. I'm working hard in this final quarter, making decisions as they arise. Once the season concludes, I will rest in the final summary judgment of the Supreme Justice.

Signed, Boots-on-the-Ground

> *Lord, give me Your strength,*
> *wisdom, and fortitude today.*

Reflect: Is there anyone questioning your caregiving decisions? Journal briefly to express your feelings and ask the Lord to shower His grace upon you. God sees your labors, dear friend.

42.

This Magic Moment

And God did extraordinary miracles.

– Acts 19:11

Over the years our youngest sons, William and Trevor, spent many happy childhood days with my parents. Will was sixteen when his grandfather died and Trevor eight years old. Both grieved deeply as their weekly visits with Pop were cut short and Gigi's role changed.

The year prior, Trevor had begun teaching himself card tricks, eventually advancing to simple illusion-type magic shows. Always eager for a new audience, Trevor practiced his magic acts on Mom and the hospice staff that came to the house. The nurse manager especially enjoyed his antics and dubbed him "The Great Trevini."

After every trick, Trevor would ask, "Want to know how I did it?" His delight at presenting magic included divulging the method behind every trick.

But something truly inexplicable occurred one day when William stopped by for lunch. Sitting around Mom's familiar kitchen table to enjoy some hearty sandwiches, we paused first to pray. I absent-mindedly asked Mom to offer a blessing, forgetting that she now spoke only a couple words at a time.

What happened next caused my eyes to meet Will's in astonishment as we heard Mom offer a fluent prayer of thanksgiving to God for food and family. It was a miraculous moment, and I love the fact that Mom's last sentences on earth were offered in prayer.

Dear Lord, thank you for Your mysterious ways – how a child can bring comfort to the aging and how the Holy Spirit can speak forth from one's heart.

Reflect: Can you think of an everyday miracle that God has done for you amidst your caregiving? Hold out to Him a "big cup" and ask for more.

43.

Going with a Pro

Plans are established by taking advice.

—Proverbs 20:18 (NRSVCE)

Mom and Dad as a couple were challenged when it came to house décor and clearly had never read *Home Decorating for Dummies*. Mom liked pinks and blues while Dad preferred browns and greens. In addition, they owned an incongruous assortment of paintings, pottery, and tapestries given them by missionaries over the years, which created a peculiar mishmash which I would describe as traditional-Asian-country-African.

Looking ahead to when I would be selling Mom's house, I pondered what preparation might be helpful. "Undecorating" the rooms inside would likely upset Mom, but what about the outside? I thought of the faded red-violet shutters and the plain white front door, and then I thought of Julia.

A reasonably-priced interior decorator, Julia had helped me with my own home in the past. Understanding that not everyone could afford full-fledged design services, Julia would offer paint color suggestions and expert ideas, but then leave the painting, purchasing, and arranging to the client.

We stood together in the driveway, Julia and I, sizing up my parents' split-level home. She noted the colorful flagstone leading to the front door as well as the ivory stucco and offered suggestions as I held out a plastic ring of shutter choices and a brochure of paint colors. Julia chose deep blue for the shutters and a dark red wine color for the front door. Shutters in a color that would suit Mom and a front door color that Dad would have liked. Perfect!

*Lord, thank you for kind professionals
who help us move plans forward.*

Reflect: Does your loved one have a favorite color? Think of a way you can place that color before them.

44.

Two Moms and a Memory

Even to your old age I am he, even when your hair is gray I will carry you.

—Isaiah 46:4 (NABRE)

She called my mom her "angel" during the years that her husband, Jack, was bedridden. For seven years, my mother-in-law, Morry, cared for Jack at home with the help of family and a nursing agency. When Jack's catheter would clog and emergency visits from the agency were not forthcoming, Morry would call Mom. A retired nurse, Mom would drop everything and drive over to adeptly solve the problem at hand.

That was 25 years ago and now, with both husbands gone and aging taking its toll, months had passed since Mom and Morry had seen one another. I sensed that life's seasons were turning and took Mom over to Morry's house for a visit.

Despite the hot August summer afternoon, the perpetual pot of tea was brewing in Morry's kitchen.

I don't recall if Mom accepted a cup of tea, but she definitely received Morry's kind, loving care. Although Morry was nearing ninety, dementia didn't run in her family. Perhaps that's why she was so saddened to see Mom's mind failing. "She's so young," Morry would say.

Here sat two very different women, raised in different families, who viewed life through different lenses—brought together by the marriage of their children and communing together one last time. Amen.

*Lord, thank you when loved ones
can bring comfort in difficult times.*

Reflect: Do you have a friend or relative in the area who truly cares about you? How has that person expressed care for you?

Part V

THE FINAL SEASON

45.

Club Med

The Lord created medicines from the earth,
and a sensible man will not despise them.

—Sirach 38:4

"Who prescribed that for her?" Mom's geriatrician asked during a routine checkup some weeks after my father's death.

The prescription had been ordered the evening before Dad's funeral when I had called requesting medication to keep Mom calm throughout the service and burial. The doctor-on-call prescribed a drug that successfully minimized Mom's anxiety; I was grateful. With agitation and nervousness being an Alzheimer's norm for Mom, we continued giving her this medicine daily after the funeral. Although not an opiate, it was known to become habit-forming.

Mom's geriatrician reluctantly continued the prescription, but at a level that required rationing. *For an octogenarian with advancing Alzheimer's, what difference does it make?* I thought to myself. *The medication eases the day-to-day for her and her caregivers!* Buying a pill-cutter, I gave Mom quarter portions as necessary to prevent running out.

At the next appointment, I asked the doctor about his anti-med approach, and he responded saying that all drugs are potentially deadly. His position frustrated me because I knew that Mom would be heavily medicated if living in a care facility. For a daughter trying to keep her mother at home, this physician offered little empathy or practical support!

With hospice in place, things had immediately improved. A simple phone call to the nurse manager, and the needed medication was delivered, thus keeping Mom much more comfortable and easing the job of her caregivers.

I felt angry at my mother's doctor—a geriatrician who, in my opinion, made in-home caregiving more difficult than was necessary.

> *Lord, please remove my anger. Give all doctors empathy, and thank you for hospice care.*

Reflect: Do you feel angry at anyone right now? Ask the Lord to diffuse the anger and to provide for your needs.

46.

Bed Climb

He lay down to sleep, resting his head on a stone.

—Genesis 28:11 (GNT)

When Mom and Dad became empty-nesters, they hired a contractor to renovate the spacious attic area of their home, raising the roof and adding large windows, closets, and a small bathroom. The result was a master bedroom that felt like sleeping in a treehouse.

After Dad's death, Mom continued climbing the six steps to this attic-level bedroom for both her afternoon naps and overnight sleep. I found it a pleasant place to help Mom each morning. After her shower, I would place a chair by the window and blow dry Mom's hair using a round brush. She had naturally wavy and full hair, so my styling efforts yielded nice results.

With Mom's needs increasing, I struggled to attend to her in the small bathroom. A bigger bathroom, located on the middle level, connected to a large blue bedroom. I started directing Mom to that bedroom for afternoon naps, and she obediently complied, but at night insisted on the attic bedroom.

Rather than fight, I placed the two massive wooden dining room table inserts atop the bed in the attic room thinking this would deter Mom. You can imagine my surprise the next evening when, after tidying up the kitchen, I headed upstairs to find Mom lying atop the table inserts!

The next day, my husband replaced the attic bedroom doorknob with a lockable knob. When Mom tried the door and found it locked, she compliantly turned and went into the blue bedroom.

*Help us and our loved ones to adjust, Lord,
as we adapt to their changing needs.*

Reflect: What changes have you made recently to accommodate your loved one? Ask the Lord for extra grace amidst the changes.

47.

Choosing Chocolate

Carry down to the man a present, a little balm and a little honey, gum, myrrh, pistachio nuts, and almonds.

—Genesis 43:11

My mother had a sign hanging in her kitchen that read, "I'd give up chocolate, but I'm no quitter." Mom loooved chocolate. If stumped on birthday gift ideas for her, a box of good quality chocolate was an easy choice.

But now was a different season. I'd been minding Mom for almost a year, and gift boxes of chocolate seemed a distant memory.

Mom was napping often and although she still ate the meals I placed in front of her, she was struggling to swallow her pills. The hospice aide recommended a cream version of one medication, but that was just one.

Then I thought of chocolate. Going to the store, I purchased a box of butter creams—Mom's favorites.

Taking one, I embedded a couple of pills deep into the middle. "Here's some chocolate, Mom," I said. She readily opened her mouth and with pleasure chewed and swallowed the entire piece and its contents. Voila! I also learned, when giving her just one small pill, I could place it in a spoonful of ice cream for the desired result.

I love to think that some of the very last food Mom ate was her beloved chocolate.

Lord, please give us creative ways to solve even the small problems we encounter when caregiving.

Reflect: As the caregiving days continue, is there something that is becoming more difficult for your loved one to do? Ask the Lord for creative solutions.

48.

Placement Puzzle

*The LORD will guard your coming
and going both now and forever.*

—Psalm 121:8 (NAB)

I followed the admissions person down the hall toward the memory-care unit. "We don't have any unoccupied single rooms, but there is one bed available in a shared room," she said over her shoulder. We approached some double doors where she typed a code into the nearby keypad, and the doors swung open. I followed her through the doors for a tour of the unit.

It was September, approaching the first anniversary of my father's death. Keeping Mom in her home this past year had been like piecing together a puzzle. With my son monitoring the overnight hours, my taking the early-morning shift, and several wonderful aides, we had a every hour covered. My husband's lighter travel schedule allowed him to help at home in my absence.

That said, the stress of managing Mom's care was taking its toll on my family. In essence, I was doing two full-time jobs. If Mom had little time left, then maybe we could hold on. But she continued to be quite mobile and could conceivably live for quite some time.

Placing Mom in a senior care facility close to home would allow me to visit often but not bear the weight of her care entirely on my shoulders. After the tour, I took the admissions paperwork home and began making preparations to move Mom to the memory care unit of the senior living facility.

Lord, help us as we strive to make decisions that best serve all of our loved ones.

Reflect: Evaluate your current caregiving situation. If changes are needed, ask the Lord to give you wisdom for the next step.

49.

One Step Closer

I know, O LORD, that the way of man
is not in himself, that it is not in man
who walks to direct his steps.

—Jeremiah 10:23

My mom had dementia from Alzheimer's, but she always knew me—until one Saturday close to a year after Dad died. On this evening, when I entered the kitchen where she was eating dinner, I could tell she didn't recognize me.

I sat with Mom and her aide Joann as Mom finished up her meal. "Beth, it's time to go upstairs and get ready for bed," Joann said kindly. Mom pushed back her chair and stood up. Joann came alongside her, gently taking one arm to guide her into the next room. Mom didn't move. She wasn't being belligerent, but somehow she didn't remember how to place one foot in front of the other.

I stood and took Mom's other arm and together Joann and I gently led and persistently pushed and pulled Mom, getting her to move through the dining room and into the living room. After thirty minutes, we finally stood before the six steps leading up to the hall. And there we were stuck. Mom no longer seemed to know how to climb steps. For fifteen minutes, I kept encouraging her to lift her foot, to no avail. I finally pressed behind her knee, got it to bend, and manually lifted her right foot up onto the bottom step. Then I followed suit with her left knee and foot. And that's how we got Mom up the steps that night.

Lord, help us to be creative when the limits of our loved one present new challenges.

Reflect: Are the caregiving challenges you are faced with changing either gradually or suddenly? Ask the Lord to give grace amidst change.

50.

The Blues

After this I looked, and lo, in heaven an open door!

—Revelation 4:1

In later years, we called it "The Blue Room." The walls were a warm yellow color, and the shag rug, an older carpet, featured several different shades of blue mixed among the fibers.

It was the largest of the four bedrooms, the one which my sister and I once shared. In more recent years, it had been a guest bedroom for the many missionaries and friends that my parents hosted. It held a king-sized bed, large closet, and direct door to the hall bathroom.

Mom had been sleeping in this room for the last couple of months, making it easier to attend to her showering and personal needs. Things had been getting messier, and I'd already cut away half the rug, pulling it up and excising portions with a razor knife. The hardwood floor underneath was easier to wipe up.

I told the hospice deliverymen to place the hospital bed in the corner of the blue room, nearest the bathroom door. This was the very same corner where my grandmother's hospital bed had stood thirty years earlier when Mom lovingly nursed her through end-stage cancer and where she had passed away. It was the same corner where fourteen months earlier, my daughter had brought forth a baby boy in a beautiful home birth.

This room was a portal for life, both in and out of this world. Now the door to the next life was again opening—this time for my mom.

Lord, grant us Your peace as we travel the byways of life, leading us and those we love eventually to the next life.

Reflect: Do you have a favorite room in your home, or one you remember from the past? Why is that room special?

51.

Buried Treasure

When I enter my house, I shall find rest with her,
for companionship with her has no bitterness,
and life with her has no pain.

—Wisdom 8:16

As Mom's life was fading, we kept vigil by her bedside. Adjacent to Mom's hospital bed sat the king-sized bed, which allowed me to rest comfortably overnight.

During the day, Mom's faithful aide was present, and hospice staff sifted in and out—the nurse, social worker, hospice aide, chaplain. There was a grief counselor on call, who promised availability for an entire year after Mom died.

With a tiny syringe, we administered medication and water, squeezing them into the corner of Mom's mouth. I could hear her swallow the liquid. Also given were strong painkillers to ease her moments of agitation and restlessness.

In the afternoon came a lull as Mom slept. Feeling weary, I stretched out beneath the bedspread of the king-sized bed and closed my eyes.

My daughter entered the room and sat quietly at the bedside of her beloved "Gigi." After a time, she approached the king-sized bed and lifted the bedspread. Then, my daughter climbed in beside me. We spoke not, but just lay beneath the cover, our mutual grief providing a blanket of comfort and support. She remained there with me for an hour or more as I recalled times she'd spent as a child with Gigi—playing, painting, eating popcorn, and for six months as a teenager, living in one of the bedrooms here. Deep within all of us, gentle transitions were taking place.

Thank you, Lord, that amidst the loss
of a loved one there can be relational gain.

Reflect: Think of your loved one's family members, whether they live near or far. If there is any discord, pray for healing.

52.

Caregiving 365

They bring thank offerings to the house of the Lord.

—Jeremiah 33:11

"She looked so peaceful and at rest," the funeral director said while we were making arrangements for the interment of my mother's body. *Wow,* I thought, *He sees a lot of dead people. The difference in Mom must have been remarkable.*

I recalled Mom's final hours a couple days earlier. Physically, she was clean and comfortable, thanks to hospice help. Spiritually, she had hope due to her deep Christian faith, and emotionally she looked forward to seeing Dad in heaven. Mom had fought the good earthly fight, keeping on through hard times.

My sister lived two thousand miles away but had now arrived to keep vigil with me during Mom's last days. Even though my sister didn't profess faith in the Lord, it was her idea to sing *Amazing Grace.* While we sang, Mom peacefully passed away.

After Dad's death a year earlier, caregiving responsibilities had careened down upon me. The relentless demands were both hands-on and administrative. Nine months into non-stop days brought about some wise advice, and I realized something needed to change. "Lord," I prayed, "Mom loves being at home, but I can't do this much longer. When the year anniversary of Dad's death comes, I will place Mom in a care facility." I comforted myself at the time, thinking at least I'd have kept Mom at home for an entire year.

The paperwork to admit Mom to a nursing home was on my desk when she suddenly suffered rapid decline. And Mom entered glory on a Sunday morning—exactly 365 days after Dad.

*Thank you, Lord, for hearing
and answering our prayers.*

Reflect: Get honest with God about your caregiving journey. Ask the Lord to show His hand in a clear way.

Epilogue

The Chosen Campground

They crossed the Jordan and camped.

—2 Samuel 24:5 (GNT)

Mom and Dad's old 26-foot camper sat in the driveway alongside their house. When I unlocked the side door, pulled out the metal step and climbed in, the familiar smell evoked sweet memories and a few tears.

I recalled Dad expressing guilt over the camper's cost, wondering if it was a wise expenditure. "But it makes Mom so happy," he would say. Mom loved getaways and called the camper her "Vacation Home."

Dad loved making Mom happy. Fossilized in my brain were his words from the day I'd asked his wishes if he were to die first. "Keep her at home, where she's comfortable," he had said. *I did, Dad, by God's grace.*

The time had come to sell the camper. My husband lifted the hood and chuckled at the discovery of a rusty tin can covering the leaky exhaust system. Dad had been known for his creative, inexpensive solutions to problems. I began cleaning out the inside of the camper. In a pouch behind the driver's seat, I discovered a list of Mom's favorite campgrounds. It brought to mind the last line of a spiritual song, and I began singing softly, "I want to cross over into campground."[1]

Dad and Mom each had crossed over their final river—exactly one year apart. Even though I sorely missed them, no doubt they were now in Mom's most-desired campground of all.

Thank you, Lord, that to be absent in the body is to be present with You.

Reflect: Your faithfulness as a caregiver is seen by God. Take heart, for He knows the future, holds you in the palm of His hand, and is preparing a mansion for you in your heavenly home.

---

[1] "Deep River." Hymnary.org. https://hymnary.org/text/deep_river_my_home_is_over_jordan.

A Note from the Author

Dear Reader,

Thank you for reading my caregiving story. I hope it encourages you in your own story. For more devotional moments, visit Olive Tree blog where I publish weekly One-Minute Photo Devotions!

In faith and friendship,

Lisa Livezey

Olive Tree Blog

"But as for me, I am like a green olive tree in the house of God; my trust is in the tender mercy of God forever and ever."
—***Psalm 52:9***

OLIVE TREES SYMBOLIZE PEACE, WISDOM, AND ENDURANCE. EACH 1-MINUTE PHOTO DEVOTION FEATURES AN ORIGINAL PHOTO WITH A SCRIPTURE, PRAYER, QUOTE, AND TAKEAWAY THOUGHT. BE BLESSED!

WWW.LISALIVEZEY.COM/OLIVETREE

KEEP IN TOUCH WITH LISA LIVEZEY

 lisalivezeywriter

 Lisa Livezey

 Lisa Livezey

 lisa@lisalivezey.com

PLEASE SUBSCRIBE TO LISA'S
1-MINUTE PHOTO DEVOTIONS FOR
WEEKLY INSPIRATION

https://www.lisalivezey.com/about-1

AND CONSIDER LEAVING A REVIEW ON
GOODREADS AND AMAZON TO SPREAD THE
WORD ABOUT—

MINDING MOM:
A CAREGIVER'S DEVOTIONAL STORY

www.ingramcontent.com/pod-product-compliance
Lightning Source LLC
LaVergne TN
LVHW020932090426
835512LV00020B/3327